# CONFRONTING STEREOTYPES

## Other Books in the LIVING PROUD! Series

# CONFRONTING STEREOTYPES

*Robert Rodi and Laura Ross*

Foreword by Kevin Jennings
Founder, GLSEN (the Gay, Lesbian & Straight
Education Network)

MASON CREST

Mason Crest
450 Parkway Drive, Suite D
Broomall, PA 19008
www.masoncrest.com

Printed in the United States of America

9 8 7 6 5 4 3 2

Series ISBN: 978-1-4222-3501-0
Hardcover ISBN: 978-1-4222-3509-6
ebook ISBN: 978-1-4222-8382-0

Cataloging-in-Publication Data is available on file at the Library of Congress.


**Developed and Produced by** Print Matters Productions, Inc. (www.printmattersinc.com)
**Cover and Interior Design by** Kris Tobiassen, Matchbook Digital

**Picture credits:** 10, LivingImages/iStock; 13, Judy Tejero Photography/Fotolia; 14, Wikimedia Creative Commons; 16, Marie-Lan Nguyen/Wikimedia Creative Commons; 20, nini/iStock; 22, Wikimedia Creative Commons; 25, NET Television; 30, Jason Doly/iStock; 32, Creatista/iStock; 36, Warner Brothers/Album/Newscom; 39, PR Photos; 41, Erika Cross/Shutterstock; 43, Creative Commons; 46, Dave Bedrosian/ZUMA Press/Newscom; 49, Bill Wilson/Wikimedia Creative Commons; 52, Joe Schildhorn/BFA/Sipa USA/Newscom; 57, Arrow Studio/Fotolia
**Front cover:** FotografiaBasica/iStock

# CONFRONTING STEREOTYPES

# CONTENTS

## KEY ICONS TO LOOK FOR

 **Text-Dependent Questions:** These questions send the reader back to the text for more careful attention to the evidence presented there.

 **Words to Understand:** These words with their easy-to-understand definitions will increase the reader's understanding of the text while building vocabulary skills.

 **Series Glossary of Key Terms:** This back-of-the-book glossary contains terminology used throughout this series. Words found here increase the reader's ability to read and comprehend higher-level books and articles in this field.

 **Research Projects:** Readers are pointed toward areas of further inquiry connected to each chapter. Suggestions are provided for projects that encourage deeper research and analysis.

 **Sidebars:** This boxed material within the main text allows readers to build knowledge, gain insights, explore possibilities, and broaden their perspectives by weaving together additional information to provide realistic and holistic perspectives.

# FOREWORD

I loved libraries as a kid.

Every Saturday my mom and I would drive from the trailer where we lived on an unpaved road in the unincorporated town of Lewisville, North Carolina, and make the long drive to the "big city" of Winston-Salem to go to the downtown public library, where I would spend joyous hours perusing the books on the shelves. I'd end up lugging home as many books as my arms could carry and generally would devour them over the next seven days, all the while eagerly anticipating next week's trip. The library opened up all kinds of worlds to me—all kinds of worlds, except a gay one.

Oh, I found some "gay" books, even in the dark days of the 1970s. I'm not sure how I did, but I found my way to authors like Tennessee Williams, Yukio Mishima, and Gore Vidal. While these great artists created masterpieces of literature that affirmed that there were indeed other gay people in the universe, their portrayals of often-doomed gay men hardly made me feel hopeful about my future. It was better than nothing, but not much better. I felt so lonely and isolated I attempted to take my own life my junior year of high school.

In the 35 years since I graduated from high school in 1981, much has changed. Gay–straight alliances (an idea my students and I pioneered at Concord Academy in 1988) are now widespread in American schools. Out LGBT (lesbian, gay, bisexual, and transgender) celebrities and programs with LGBT themes are commonplace on the airwaves. Oregon has a proud bisexual governor, multiple members of Congress are out as lesbian, gay, or bisexual, and the White House was bathed in rainbow colors the day marriage equality became the law of the land in 2015. It gets better, indeed.

So why do we need the Living Proud! series?

- Because GLSEN (the Gay, Lesbian & Straight Education Network) reports that over two-thirds of LGBT students routinely hear anti-LGBT language at school

- Because GLSEN reports that over 60% of LGBT students do not feel safe at school
- Because the CDC (the Centers for Disease Control and Prevention, a U.S. government agency) reports that lesbian and gay students are four times more likely to attempt suicide than heterosexual students

In my current role as the executive director of the Arcus Foundation (the world's largest financial supporter of LGBT rights), I work in dozens of countries and see how far there still is to go. In over 70 countries same-sex relations are crimes under existing laws: in 8, they are a crime punishable by the death penalty. It's better, but it's not all better—especially in our libraries, where there remains a need for books that address LGBT issues that are appropriate for young people, books that will erase both the sense of isolation so many young LGBT people still feel as well as the ignorance so many non-LGBT young people have, ignorance that leads to the hate and violence that still plagues our community, both at home and abroad.

The Living Proud! series will change that and will save lives. By providing accurate, age-appropriate information to young people of all sexual orientations and gender identities, the Living Proud! series will help young people understand the complexities of the LGBT experience. Young LGBT people will see themselves in its pages, and that reflection will help them see a future full of hope and promise. I wish Living Proud! had been on the shelves of the Winston-Salem/Forsyth County Public Library back in the seventies. It would have changed my life. I'm confident that it will have as big an impact on its readers today as it would have had on me back then. And I commend it to readers of any age.

Kevin Jennings
Founder, GLSEN (the Gay, Lesbian & Straight Education Network)
Executive Director, Arcus Foundation

**GLSEN®**

GLSEN is the leading national education organization focused on ensuring safe and affirming schools for all students. GLSEN seeks to develop school climates where difference is valued for the positive contribution it makes to creating a more vibrant and diverse community. www.glsen.org

Gay people are as diverse as the general population. Stereotypes can be very confusing, making you feel like you have to conform to a set image that is not who you are.

# 1

# WHAT ARE STEREOTYPES?

 **WORDS TO UNDERSTAND**

**Transgender:** Identifying with a different gender than the one that was assigned at birth (i.e., a person designated as male who identifies as female or vice-versa).
**Standardized:** Made to conform to a set of rules.
**Generalizations:** Vague opinions not based on specific facts.
**Flamboyantly:** In a manner that is colorful and a bit outrageous.
**Butch:** Masculine in dress and appearance.
**Disparaging:** Negative and rather insulting.
**Effeminate:** A man who looks or acts in ways that are considered feminine.

Ed Wesley remembers what it was like before he came out and told the world he was gay. He felt alone and out of place. Everything he knew about the lesbian, gay, bisexual, and **transgender** (LGBT) community came from the characters he'd seen on television and the way gay people were portrayed in the media. To him, it seemed like all gay men squealed like girls, were obsessed with body image, wore women's clothing, and talked with a lisp.

That wasn't Ed.

"I'm not a skinny little gay boy," he says. "I'm a big guy. I'm not like the characters they show on television or on the news. So for a little while, that made me wonder if I was gay, because I didn't fit the way I was supposed to. I thought I was supposed to be something else. It was confusing."

When Ed finally realized that being gay didn't mean he would have to fit into a set image, he felt more comfortable with himself and his sexual identity. He was able to embrace his homosexuality and come out. But he isn't the only gay person who has been confused by the stereotypes that exist in modern culture.

According to the *Merriam-Webster* dictionary, a stereotype is a **standardized** mental picture that is held in common by members of a group and that represents an oversimplified opinion, prejudiced attitude, or uncritical judgment. Put more simply, it's when someone defines an entire group of people by just a few characteristics. In most cases, stereotypes are negative or highlight only the most extreme elements of the group. They overlook the more complex aspects of the individual people that make up the group.

"I'm much more than just a gay stereotype," says Wesley. "All people are more than the **generalizations** we sometimes give them. I hate when people do it to me, but I realize that I do it to other people, too."

This is the stereotypical image we often have in our minds when we hear the word "nerd."

 ## CLOSE-UP: SOME COMMON HIGH SCHOOL STEREOTYPES

The average high school has its share of stereotypes—lumping certain kinds of people together, ignoring the ways that each person is unique. These stereotypes are often expressed with a single word or phrase: jock, nerd, goth, prep, geek. The images these words call to mind are easily recognized and understood by others who share the same views, but they don't tell the whole story about an individual. A person's most interesting qualities may be overlooked when he or she is lumped into a stereotype.

## Butch Women, Effeminate Men

Stereotypes exist for many different groups. Thinking that all black people can dance well or that all Japanese students are geniuses are examples of stereotypes. Conforming to a stereotype isn't necessarily a bad thing. There's nothing wrong with dancing well or being very smart. The problem comes when someone ignores who a person *really is* and instead only thinks about the stereotypes.

The cartoon character Speedy Gonzales presented an insulting image of Mexicans.

Sometimes stereotypes can be truly harmful. In 1999, the cartoon character Speedy Gonzales was taken off the air because many experts believed that he and his fellow mouse characters perpetuated stereotypes of Mexicans. According to this stereotype—if every Mexican really were like Speedy—all Mexicans have thick accents, are often drunk, and tend to be lazy. Some people felt canceling the cartoon was extreme, but for many children, Speedy was their introduction to Mexican culture—and it meant they started out life with a warped (and false) perception of Mexicans.

"Stereotypes hurt people," says Brian Jones, an out gay black man. "Whether they're based on race or culture or sexual orientation. Even if it's meant as a joke or just to be funny, some people take it seriously. And when that happens, the problems can start, because some people don't realize that it's a joke or even a stereotype. They think it's fact and true."

When people think of the LGBT community, they often envision the many stereotypes that have become common in entertainment and the media. Many, especially those who don't personally know any LGBT individuals, think all gay people conform to stereotypes—starting with the idea that gay men behave like women and gay women behave like men.

"When I saw what I thought gay people were—what the stereotypes were—I was scared because I didn't fit into it," says openly gay writer Fred Carlton. "I thought I would have to change who I was just so I could be gay. And that doesn't make any sense at all. I thought I was going to have to be more like a woman, and I don't want to be a woman! I can be sensitive and creative while still being a man."

Drag queens are colorful figures but are only one of the nearly infinite shades of gay.

## Where Stereotypes Come From

Stereotypes of the LGBT community often confuse a person's sexual orientation with his or her gender identity. When someone is physically attracted to a member of the same sex, that is his or her *sexual orientation*. It doesn't mean gay men are more feminine than straight men, nor that gay women are more masculine than straight women.

 **CLOSE-UP: SEX VERSUS GENDER**

You may think that gender and sex mean the same thing—but actually, they are two different things. According to the World Health Organization, "sex" refers to the biological and physiological characteristics that define men and women, whereas "gender" refers to the socially constructed roles, behaviors, activities, and attributes that a society considers appropriate for men and women.

To put it another way: "Male" and "female" are sex categories, whereas "masculine" and "feminine" are gender categories.

Aspects of sex will not vary substantially between different human societies, but aspects of gender may vary greatly.

To be clear, sexual orientation is not directly related to gender identity. Sexual orientation refers to one's physical and emotional attraction to the same sex, the opposite sex, or both sexes. Gender identity, on the other hand, refers to someone's self-identity as either male, female, or something different. Does this sound confusing? It really just means that the relationship between sexual orientation and gender can vary.

But sometimes stereotypes are true. After all, they come from some-where, even when they may be exaggerated. Many people know or have seen **flamboyantly** gay men or tough **butch** lesbians. LGBT pride fes-tivals and parades sometimes showcase members of the community who fulfill certain stereotypes. But the mistake many people make is to think that these stereotypes describe what *all* LGBT people are like or how they behave.

"Stereotypes are what keep people in the closet," Wesley says. "They aren't what we can be or even what we want to be."

As was the case when Wesley was coming out, stereotypes can be con-fusing to individuals who are questioning their sexual or gender identity especially if they don't know any LGBT people. They may already feel out of place among their peers, and they may not feel that they fit in with LGBT stereotypes, either. They may be embarrassed to associate them-selves with some of the **disparaging** stereotypes that have been linked to LGBT people.

"I don't want someone to look at me and just see a black man or just see a gay man," says Jones. "I want them to see Brian, the person I am. I don't swish when I walk. I'm not a rapper. I do some things that are considered 'black' and I do things that are considered 'gay.' But I also do hundreds of other things. I'm more than just a stereotype."

**TEXT-DEPENDENT QUESTIONS**

- Are sexual orientation and gender identity related?

- Do stereotypes have any basis in reality?

- What is the difference between sex and gender?

 **RESEARCH PROJECTS**

- Think about the ways you yourself might stereotype LGBT people, or the ways you might stereotype other minorities.

- Pay close attention to the marchers in the next LGBT pride parade in your area; look for evidence that those who embody stereotypes are either behaving true to character or are acting that way *theatrically*—for effect.

- Talk to older, out LGBT people. Ask them about how stereotypes affected their coming-out processes.

Certain occupations, such as dancer, are often assumed to be filled by gay men. This stereotype is not only unfair to gay people in general but also to the straight people who choose these careers.

# 2

# STEREOTYPES OF GAY MEN

 **WORDS TO UNDERSTAND**

**Caricature:** An exaggerated representation of a person, usually created to make people laugh.
**Activist:** Someone who takes action on behalf of a particular cause.
**Homophobic:** Something that perpetuates fear and hatred of gay people.
**Proliferate:** Increase or multiply.

In the classic nineties comedy *Clueless*, a character describes a gay class-mate as "a disco-dancing, Oscar Wilde-reading, Streisand ticket-holding friend of Dorothy." His friend adds, "He does like to shop . . . and the boy can dress."

They were referring to some of the most common stereotypes asso-ciated with gay men—: they enjoy dancing at clubs, behave like openly gay 19th-century writer Oscar Wilde, and are fans of the singer Barbara

Streisand and the actress Judy Garland, who portrayed Dorothy in *The Wizard of Oz* (thus, "friend of Dorothy"). It's also said that gay men enjoy shopping and have an excellent sense of style and fashion.

"We all love Cher. We all love Marilyn Monroe," says Tom Boller, an openly gay architect in New York City. "We prance and mince and clap our hands and say things like, 'That's fabulous!' That's what people think. And when you look on television or [in] movies, that's what it seems like. But that's not how it really is. I play soccer every weekend. I don't know anything about Marilyn Monroe. I never say 'fabulous.'"

Oscar Wilde was a 19th-century British writer known for his flamboyant homosexuality.

## We're Not All Hairdressers, Dancers, or Wedding Planners

There are certain occupations that tend to be thought of as "gay." Hairdressers, interior decorators, florists, dancers, and stage actors are all jobs stereotypically thought to be filled by gay men. Such stereotypes affect not only all gay people, but also the straight people who choose these careers.

"People assume that if you're a male ballet dancer, you're gay," says Zach Hench, a straight professional dancer from Philadelphia. "And I think it's quite silly because let's think about it—you are working around beautiful women all day that are half naked. It's a great job for straight guys."

"I know gay lawyers, gay doctors, gay teachers, gay coaches, gay athletes, gay accountants," says Boller. "We're not all wedding planners and pet groomers. Those are just the silly stereotypes that people see in movies and on TV. But if they don't know any actual gay people, then they don't know better."

 **CLOSE-UP: GAY VOICE**

One of the ways gay men are most often stereotyped is by the way they sound. For decades, stand-up comics would mimic gay men by adopting a lilting, lisping manner of speech. Today, this is obviously considered politically incorrect; however, on the premise that every stereotype has a foundation in reality, gay men have recently begun to consider whether there is in fact a difference in the way many of them speak, and whether it's innate or something learned. The most highly publicized exploration of this phenomenon is filmmaker David Thorpe's documentary *Do I Sound Gay?*, which features such celebrities as Tim Gunn, Dan Savage, and George Takei addressing the question.

Hollywood has often been guilty of presenting and even creating stereotypes. Countless movies show flamboyantly gay characters who get laughs with their stereotypical behavior. The popular sitcom *Will & Grace* was a huge step forward for gay and lesbian people on television, but many felt the show didn't do a good enough job of showing diversity within the gay community. The gay characters of Will and Jack were often obsessed with appearances, money, and fashion. They made jokes about lesbians, bisexuals, and transgender people, showing how the gay community can often be as guilty of stereotyping as the rest of the world. Jack, in particular, was a **caricature** of gay stereotypes: an out-of-work actor who worshiped Cher and used pop culture references as he dished out catty jibes to his friends.

"I don't care if he's rich or poor, fat or thin," said Jack, describing his ideal mate. "As long as he's rich and thin."

Such characters are common in popular culture. Television, movies, and theater frequently feature prancing, limp-wristed gay men who fill the role of the stylish sidekick.

"Those flaming gay characters are funny. I laugh at them!" says Todd Ramos, a gay **activist**. "And I don't think there's anything wrong with them when it comes to entertainment. But the problem is that some people think that's what all gay people are like, or when they think that's *all* gay people are."

Some stereotypes can also be very damaging in other ways. In the 1980s, due to the high number of homosexual men infected with HIV, the virus that causes AIDS, people often considered it a gay disease. That led to the stereotype that all gay men have AIDS.

"That's probably one of the worst," Ramos says. "I remember when I told my mother I was gay, and that was the first thing she said. She was scared I would get AIDS. And it didn't come from a hateful place. It was just because she didn't know any better. She believed what she saw on television."

## The Stereotype Trap

Another negative effect of stereotypes is that they are difficult to escape. This was the case for Sean Hayes, who played Jack on *Will & Grace* for the show's eight seasons and came out publicly in 2010. As one of the

The television series *Will & Grace* was considered to be groundbreaking in many ways for the LGBT community, but it also perpetuated some gay stereotypes. Sean Hayes, who played the character Jack, is on the far left.

WILL & GRACE  NBT

increasing number of openly LGBT actors in Hollywood, Hayes was then faced with the question of whether he would be able to play straight characters. The stereotypically flamboyant Jack, his most famous and recognized role, had come to define his identity.

Hayes was at the center of public controversy when *Newsweek*'s Ramin Setoodeh reviewed his performance in the Broadway stage play *Promises, Promises*, in which Hayes played a straight leading man. In his review, Setoodeh wrote that Hayes's history of having played a gay character, along with his personal sexual orientation, made it difficult to believe he was a straight character in the play.

"Hayes is among Hollywood's best verbal slapstickers, but his sexual orientation is part of who he is, and also part of his charm," Setoodeh wrote. "But frankly, it's weird seeing Hayes play straight."

Immediately, people reacted strongly to the controversial viewpoint, particularly because Setoodeh himself is gay. Hayes's co-star in the play, actress Kristin Chenoweth, was furious at what she called a **"homophobic"** article. She responded with a written statement defending her on-stage love interest:

> *This article offends me because I am a human being, a woman, and a Christian . . . . For example, there was a time when Jewish actors had to change their names because anti-Semites thought no Jew could convincingly play a Gentile. Setoodeh even goes so far as to justify his knee-jerk homophobic reaction to gay actors by accepting and endorsing that "as viewers, we are molded by a society obsessed with dissecting sexuality, starting with the locker room torture in junior high school." Really? We*

*want to maintain and* **proliferate** *the same kind of bullying that makes children cry and in some recent cases have even taken their own lives?*

Soon, numerous stage and screen actors and writers joined Chenoweth's outrage, including Oscar-winning screenwriter Dustin Lance Black. The Gay and Lesbian Alliance Against Defamation (GLAAD), which monitors the way LGBT people are portrayed in entertainment and media, also expressed disappointment with the homophobic attitude.

"We must move beyond stereotypes," GLAAD President Jarrett Barrios wrote about the article. "As a gay man, Setoodeh should know that not all gay men are **effeminate**, nor are all lesbians masculine. Actors are hired to play a part and their sexual orientation should have no bearing on how well they can do so."

Not only did Setoodeh's perspective imply that gay actors should be limited to playing only gay roles, but it also indicated that heterosexual men couldn't behave like Hayes and still be considered straight. This is what can make stereotypes so damaging. They can make people afraid of being who they really are. Stereotypes are just another way of separating people into categories of what's "normal" and what's not.

"Seriously, why can't straight men dress well and like Madonna?" says Joe Duarte, a straight man who works with many gay men in the travel industry. "People think I'm gay all the time. I consider it a compliment. Gay guys I know look good, and they are nice, friendly guys. So I'm not insulted. But it's crazy to say that one way of talking or dressing or even gesturing is gay or straight. We're all just people. Why can't people just be who they are?"

### CLOSE-UP: GAY BEARS AND OTHER STEREOTYPE-BUSTERS

*Bear* is LGBT slang for a segment of the gay community that doesn't exactly fit many people's stereotypes of how gay men look and behave. Bears tend to be big, beefy men with facial hair, and they project an image of traditional masculinity in the way they dress and carry themselves. Much more likely to be seen in jeans, boots, and a flannel shirt than the latest fashion, Bears have a "regular guy" image that contradicts the stereotype that all gay men are feminine. Bears are masculine-identified men who happen to like other men. Most Bears are proud to call themselves gay men and to represent the gay community to the world in their own unique way. ("Where the Bears Are," a popular comedy–mystery web series set in the Bear community, has run several seasons to date.)

In fact, Bears are now so numerous that they've spawned two additional subcultures, Otters (more slender than traditional Bears, but in every other way similar) and Cubs (younger Bears). And there are various other gay groups that aren't stereotypically effeminate. Jocks, for example, are athletic gay men who participate in team sports. There is also a long-standing gay subculture devoted to leather and motorcycles. When Leather-men appear together in caps and boots, jackets and sunglasses, oozing testosterone, it's easy to mistake them at first glance for police officers.

It should be noted, however, that gay identities can be relatively fluid. Your average Bear might also be an opera fanatic, while any given Leatherman might be an avid gardener. In gay culture, busting one stereotype definitely doesn't create another one.

## TEXT-DEPENDENT QUESTIONS

- How does Hollywood reinforce gay stereotypes?
- How did the AIDS crisis make gay stereotyping more harmful?
- What problems do out gay actors face in their careers?

## RESEARCH PROJECTS

- Check out the latest gay characters on TV; note the ways in which they either conform to, or break away from, familiar stereotypes.
- Read some classics of gay literature from previous decades (check out the works of Patrick Dennis, Dawn Powell, Joe Keenan, and others) from previous decades to see how stereotypes shaped the lives of earlier generations.
- Investigate other gay subcultures; see how many different ones you can find.

Every lesbian is an individual, and no stereotype can fully encompass your full self.

# 3

# STEREOTYPES OF LESBIANS

 **WORDS TO UNDERSTAND**

**Compensating:** Making up for something by trying harder or going further in the opposite direction.
**Assumption:** A conclusion drawn without the benefit of real evidence.

She must be a lesbian.

That was a common attitude when a photo surfaced in 2010 of Supreme Court nominee Elena Kagan playing softball. The picture, which simply showed her holding a bat standing over home plate, prompted rumors that she was gay. While her sexual orientation should be irrelevant to her competency as a judge, this response illustrated the stereotype that simply playing a particular sport means a woman is a lesbian.

"I think it's unfortunate," Lisa Fernandez, a three-time Olympic gold medalist and assistant coach at the University of California Los Angeles, says of the stereotype. "It's part of our game."

Jessica Mendoza won two Olympic gold medals, but when she first began playing softball, she was surprised to learn that it was considered a lesbian sport. "There were always comments about sexuality being associated with sports," she says. "And it caught me off guard a few times."

It is a common stereotype that one member of a lesbian couple is more "butch" or masculine, while the other is more "lipstick" or feminine. In truth, there are as many variations of lesbian couples as there are of heterosexual couples.

Holly Elander, a senior who plays softball at Santa Monica High School in California, also recognizes the stereotype associated with her sport. And she sees teammates **compensating** for that. "You see a lot of girls wearing makeup, a lot of girls with their hair really pretty because you can definitely tell they still want to look pretty and probably go against those stereotypes that were pinned against them," she says.

## Reclaiming Power from the Negative

Playing softball isn't the only stereotypical behavior linked to lesbianism. "Masculine" attributes, such as short hair, an aggressive walk, and the ability to fix cars and do home repairs, are often thought to be indicators that a woman is gay.

"People always make the **assumption** that I'm handy just because I'm a lesbian," says Callie Franks, who came out when she was in college. "When I first realized I was gay, I tried to fill those stereotypes. I cut my hair really short. I became an in-your-face feminist. But that wasn't me. The real me isn't tough. I'm scared of spiders. The whole hard-core dyke thing was just a phase. But the lesbian thing is here to stay."

By using the term "dyke," Franks demonstrated a way in which many people in the LGBT communities fight stereotypes: by reclaiming once-derogatory terms and diminishing their negativity. In the same way, LGBT people have claimed the word "queer" as a term defining anyone who identifies with a sexual orientation or gender role that is outside what people consider "normal."

"When we use words like 'queer' or 'dyke' or even 'fairy' and 'queen,' we take the power away from the people who use them negatively," Franks says. "We make them our own words, and then suddenly they aren't so bad any more. We turn those stereotypes around."

 **CLOSE-UP: BUTCHES ON BROADWAY**

Lesbians have become a familiar presence on TV and in movies, but butches are still seldom seen on either screen—possibly because Hollywood is uncomfortable with very masculine women (extremely feminine men are also largely unseen). On Broadway, however, butches have scored some notable successes, beginning with the career of Lea DeLaria, the joyfully butch singer and stand-up comic who became an unexpected Broadway sensation in *On the Town* (1998) and *The Rocky Horror Show* (2000), and is now one of the stars of the Netflix TV show *Orange Is the New Black*.

More recently, *Fun Home*, based on the autobiographical graphic novel by lesbian cartoonist Alison Bechdel, won the 2015 Tony Award for Best Musical. One of the show's most memorable numbers, "Ring of Keys," features Alison as a child, being bowled over by the sight of a butch delivery woman. "Your swagger and your bearing," the girl sings ecstatically, "And the just-right clothes you're wearing / Your short hair and your dungarees / And your lace-up boots / And your keys, ohhh / Your ring of keys!"

## Butch and Femme

Lesbians are also generally placed into two categories—butch women, who are given the male role, and femmes, who are considered to be more like straight women. Limiting people to two narrow roles overlooks the aspects that make each individual unique.

"If you have long hair, if you have makeup and dress in a certain way, then you can't be a lesbian," says Mary Jo Kane, director of the Tucker Center for Research on Girls & Women in Sport at the University of Minnesota. "These are the traditionally female characteristics. And they are false." In fact, the lesbian community is filled with women who occupy a place between these two extremes—as illustrated by such categories as preppy dykes, boy-babes, power dykes, and blue jean femmes. There's even the term "futch," which is specifically coined to describe women who are both femme *and* butch. In fact, it sometimes seems there are as many ways to be lesbian as there are lesbians!

 **TEXT-DEPENDENT QUESTIONS**

- How does popular culture reinforce lesbian stereotypes?
- Are terms like "dyke" and "fairy" positive or negative?
- What are two of the major lesbian stereotypes?

 **RESEARCH PROJECTS**

- Check out the latest lesbian characters on TV; note the ways in which they either conform to, or break away from, familiar stereotypes.
- Read some classics of lesbian literature from previous decades to see how stereotypes shape the lives of earlier generations.
- Investigate other lesbian subcultures; see how many different ones you can find.

Actor Marlon Brando publicly identified himself as bisexual.

# 4

# STEREOTYPES OF BISEXUAL PEOPLE

 **WORDS TO UNDERSTAND**

**Horizontal hostility:** Negative feeling among people within the same minority group.
**Innate:** Referring to characteristics that are most basic to a person; those traits with which they were born.
**Hierarchy:** An organization of things—or people—in layers of importance, with those at the top having the most status or importance.
**Legitimize:** Make acceptable to most people.
**Spectrum:** A wide range of behaviors and choices.

Gay and lesbian people often face stereotypes and discrimination from the world. But stereotypes also exist within the LGBT community.

Bisexual people are often thought of as being different from "real" gay people. Many gays and lesbians believe bisexuals are just confused or haven't made a decision to come out as completely gay.

"Isn't that just a rest stop on the road to 'homo'?" says the gay title character Will on the sitcom *Will & Grace*, when discussing the concept.

That attitude is not uncommon. Bisexuality is often considered something young people try when they are in college, as they experiment with sexuality or question their orientation. Although this may be the case for some, it is also unfairly judgmental of individuals who are trying to be themselves in what should be an accepting community.

## Gays and Lesbians as Oppressors

"The oppression that bisexuals face is wrong, whether it is coming from the gay and lesbian community or the heterosexual community," says Lowell Kane, program coordinator of Texas A&M University's LGBT Center. "**Horizontal** hostility within the LGBT community is very troubling and certainly creates a roadblock on the path toward equity. I believe that many of the misconceptions about bisexuality and bisexual people can be cleared up with education, visibility, and a willingness to openly discuss sexuality in a civil way."

Bisexual people are physically attracted to both men and women. Some researchers believe that this is much more common than most people realize or acknowledge. Broadway star Megan Mullaly, who played Karen on the television show *Will & Grace*, has spoken publicly about the fact that she is attracted to both women and men, even though the majority of her serious relationships have been with men.

"I consider myself bisexual, and my philosophy is, everyone **innately** is," she says.

Actress Megan Mullally has publically identified herself as bisexual and has spoken out on behalf of this group.

The idea that bisexual people are confused about their sexual orientation can make their lives even more difficult. Bisexual people may be shunned by the straight community because they are involved in same-sex relationships as well as by the gay community because they still are seen as partly heterosexual.

## An LGBT Pecking Order

"Within the LGBT community, there is almost a social **hierarchy**," says Casey Beck, who identified as bisexual while a student in college. "Some homosexuals believe they are somehow better than bisexuals and trans-gendered people, more sure of their identity."

In Beck's case, he eventually recognized that he was gay and no longer dates women. But he still recalls how difficult it was to be the "B" in the LGBT community. He felt pressure to prove that he belonged—just as he often felt when he tried to fit in with the heterosexual community.

"When I tell people I'm gay, the reaction is different," Beck says. "When I used to identify as bi, there's a game of twenty questions with an extra burden to explain and **legitimize** your sexuality."

## Bisexuals and Monogamy

Beck also had to deal with the stereotype that bisexual people are more likely to cheat than are other people. This mistaken assumption stems from the fact that bisexual people are attracted to both genders, which theoretically means they could be attracted to anyone.

"People always seem to think that if you're bisexual, then you can't be in a monogamous relationship," says Sara Schneider. "As if just because you could be attracted to another man or woman, you're going to act on it. But that's like saying that all gay people cheat. Or that all straight people cheat. The fact is, cheaters cheat—gay, lesbian, bisexual, or straight."

Schneider came out as a lesbian in high school, but when she was twenty-two, she met a young man whom she considered her soul mate.

Bisexuals have often had to deal with intolerance in  both the heterosexual and gay communities. Groups specifically supporting bisexuals are relatively new and growing.

Even after twenty-five years of marriage, however, she still considers herself bisexual.

"I'm married to a man, but that doesn't mean I'm straight," she says. "People really don't understand that. And it doesn't mean I would have a relationship with anyone other than my husband, man or woman. But I know I could have fallen in love with a woman and decided to spend my life with her. To me, it's about the person. If there's a connection in your heart and in your soul, then that's what matters. In my case, that's where the physical attraction comes from. I don't think everyone is like me. Some people are, and some people aren't.

"I understand why it confuses people. Not everyone gets it or even agrees with it. That's okay. It would be easier for them if I were one thing—, if I would stand up and say, 'Yes, I'm straight.' But I don't think anyone should be something they're not just because that's what someone else labels them."

 ## CLOSE-UP: THE RANGE OF SEXUAL ORIENTATION

The pioneering sex researcher Alfred Kinsey broke from popular thinking on sexuality in the 1950s, theorizing that bisexuality was much more common than previously thought. Kinsey is probably most famous for his sexual-orientation scale, which represents exclusive heterosexuality with a zero and exclusive homosexuality with a six. Some degree of bisexuality exists in people whose numbers are 1 to 5 on the scale.

In the 1980s, Kinsey's scale was updated by researcher Eli Coleman. Coleman's research broke new ground in understanding human sexuality, showing that while some people identify as either gay or straight consistently throughout their lives, a sizable proportion of people do not. Many rate themselves as bisexual on questions of desire (or near a 3 on Kinsey's scale) but maintain exclusive gay or straight relationships. In addition, some people identify as a certain sexual identity at one point in their lives and as another later on. In other words, sexual behavior and identity are not written in stone, and may shift as we encounter new people or life circumstances.

## Bisexual ≠ Confused

As people like Lowell Kane continue to spread awareness and a message of acceptance toward bisexual people through LGBT organizations, he hopes that there will be more of a recognition that bisexuality is not a

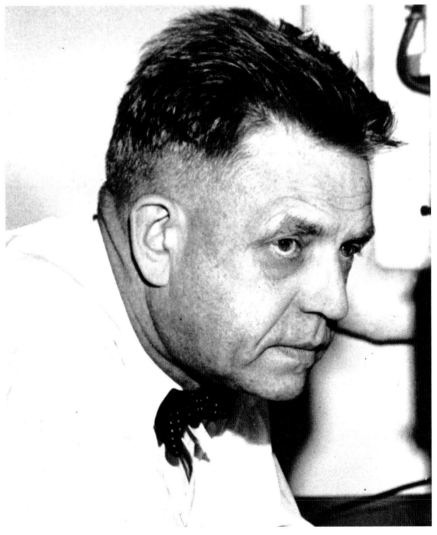

The work of sex researcher Alfred Kinsey, shown here, broke many of the stereotypes about sexual orientation that had previously existed. Kinsey himself identified as bisexual.

sign of confusion. In fact, it's probably much more common than most people realize.

"Current research suggests that sexuality is more of a fluid **spectrum** than the rigid socially constructed identities of gay, lesbian, straight, bisexual," says Kane. "These recent models of sexuality show that a large percentage (more than 30 percent) of any given population may have thoughts or feelings that fall along the bisexual spectrum, but not all will identify as bisexual because current society frowns upon any non-heterosexual orientation."

**TEXT-DEPENDENT QUESTIONS**

- How does popular culture reinforce stereotypes of bisexuals?

- How do gay and lesbian people unfairly judge bisexuals?

- Are bisexuals inclined to be less monogamous than gays and lesbians?

 **RESEARCH PROJECTS**

- Look up the Kinsey scale and determine where, from 0 to 6, you fit on it.

- Check out the latest non-heterosexual characters on TV, on such shows as *Orange Is the New Black, Transparent,* and *Call Me Caitlyn*; note the ways in which they either conform to, or break away from, familiar stereotypes.

Lana Wachowski, who along with her sister Lilly, who is also transgender, was behind such hit movies as *The Matrix* and *Cloud Atlas*. She is one of the most visible and powerful transgender people in Hollywood.

# 5

# STEREOTYPES OF TRANSGENDER PEOPLE

 **WORDS TO UNDERSTAND**

**Bell curve:** A distribution graph of data with a rounded peak that tapers away at each end, like a bell.
**Advocate:** Someone who sticks up for another person or group of people.

A group of students gathered at Penn State University to discuss some of the stereotypes that affect the lesbian, gay, bisexual, and transgender communities. During the meeting, they listed terms such as "shim," "it," and "tranny" on white marker board.

These are words often used to refer to transgender people. They are a result of the stereotype that transgender people are weird, strange, or confused about their gender.

Alex Yates, co-president of the student group that hosted the meeting, drew a diagram on the white board showing two overlapping **bell curves** representing masculinity and femininity.

"A man and a woman can be more alike than two women or two men," he said, because when following the properties of a bell curve, most people fall into the middle.

Lex Shaw, a sophomore who participated in the discussion, says she thinks gender roles are created by society, with people "pushing boys to sports and pushing girls to play with dolls."

## Stereotyping People Who Defy Stereotypes

The term *transgender* generally refers to anyone who is gender-variant, meaning they don't conform to traditional gender roles. In other words, they don't fit in with gender stereotypes.

Issues surrounding gender identity can be very complex and difficult to understand, even for the individual experiencing them. As a result, certain stereotypes have arisen, generalizing the experiences of all people who fall within the transgender category.

 **CLOSE-UP: TGs ON TV**

A pair of television shows that debuted at roughly the same time in the mid-2010s helped America better understand the transgender experience and dispel a number of stereotypes. The reality show *Call Me Caitlyn* followed the former Olympic decathlon winner Bruce Jenner in her glamorous, high-profile new female identity. Jill Soloway's comedy–drama series *Transparent* featured Jeffrey Tambor as a retired college professor with three grown children, who transitions in late middle age.

"I've worked with so many trans people, and I still don't think I understand the many distinctions and differences," says Todd Ramos, an **advocate** for LGBT rights. "But it really doesn't matter if I completely understand. What matters is that I respect people and don't try to shove my beliefs or my definitions onto them. The bottom line is that what someone else does has no effect on me. If a woman feels she fits better into the role of a man, then who am I to argue? I don't understand it, and it's certainly not how I approach the world, but that's not what matters."

Ramos believes that people have a difficult enough time understanding themselves without being influenced by other people's stereotypes

Transgender people are gaining acceptance and openness. Theresa Sparks (center) was San Francisco's first-ever transgender police commissioner. Sergeant Stephan Thorne (right) was the first transgender police officer in San Francisco. Chief Heather Fong (left) was the city's first female chief of police.

and misunderstandings. The British news website *The Guardian* features a regular column written by Juliet Jacques, who was assigned male at birth but began feeling more comfortable as a female beginning at age ten.

"I declared myself gay and a cross-dresser: 'gay' because although I felt attracted to males who were somehow female, I still considered them men; and 'cross-dresser' because it seemed the most innocuous term," Jacques says.

## Transgender ≠ Gay

The idea that transgender people are gay is a common stereotype. Some people also consider all transgender people to be drag queens, another common stereotype. Drag queens, or female impersonators, are men who wear dresses and other women's clothing for entertainment purposes. They may lip synch or dance in nightclub shows or at special events, dressing up only for their performances. This is different from being transgender which involves the authentic expression of one's internally felt gender.

"Everyone just kind of thinks that all guys who wear dresses are the same, and they're all freaks," Ramos says. "But it's ignorant to just think everyone who's different from you is a freak. Every person is different. If you take a few minutes to try to understand them, you can learn a lot. You can learn a lot about them, but you can also learn a lot about yourself, because we're all different. Being different is actually what makes us all the same."

**CLOSE-UP: TRANSVESTITE VERSUS TRANSSEXUAL**

Terms related to gender identity and sexuality can be confusing. *Transvestite* and *transsexual* are two terms that are often misused. Several differences exist between people identifying themselves as transvestites and transsexuals, although the exact definitions may vary from person to person.

One of the main differences between transvestites and transsexuals regards gender identification. Transvestites do not usually exhibit any discomfort identifying as the sex they were assigned at birth. Transvestite men want to be men; transvestite women want to be women. Many transvestites choose to adopt habits of dress or appearance associated with the opposite gender, while retaining all physical characteristics of their sex. In contrast, transsexuals believe the sex they were assigned at birth is inconsistent with their authentic gender. A transsexual may undergo chemical or anatomical alterations, including surgery, in order to conform to the physical norms of their authentic gender.

 **TEXT-DEPENDENT QUESTIONS**

- How does popular culture reinforce stereotypes of transgender people?
- How do gay and lesbian people unfairly judge transgender people?
- Is being transgender related to homosexuality?

 **RESEARCH PROJECTS**

- Take a close look at how transgender people and issues are treated in the media.
- Look further into the transgender experience (by way of biographies, essays, etc.) to help dispel your own, perhaps unsuspected, stereotypes.

Actor Alan Cumming wrote on his blog, "What's wrong with being effeminate? There are loads of straight people in the world who are effeminate."

# 6
# FIGHTING STEREOTYPES

 **WORDS TO UNDERSTAND**

**Clichés:** Ideas that have become so overused—stereotypes, for example—that they have become meaningless.
**Marginalize:** Push someone to the sidelines, away from the rest of the world.

We can't help our human tendency to put people into categories. As babies, we faced a confusing world filled with an amazing variety of new things. We needed a way to make sense of it all. One of our first steps in learning about the world around us was to sort things into separate slots in our heads: small furry things that said *meow* were kitties, while larger furry things that said *arf-arf* were doggies; cars went *vroom-vroom*, but trains were longer and went *choo-choo*; little girls looked one way and little boys another; and doctors wore white coats, while police officers wore blue.

These were our earliest stereotypes. They were a handy way to make sense of the world; they helped us know what to expect so that each time we faced a new person or thing, we weren't starting all over again from scratch. But stereotypes become dangerous when we continue to hold onto our belief in them despite new evidence. (For instance, as a child you may have decided that all dogs bite, so you were afraid of them. As you grew, you came to understand that many dogs are friendly and harmless and can be wonderful friends. If you'd hung onto your fear, you'd miss out on the pleasure of interacting with dogs.) Stereotypes are particularly dangerous and destructive when they're directed at persons or groups of persons. That's when they turn into prejudice.

"Every day, we see stereotypes of what it means to be male and female," says Callie Franks, who teaches tolerance to high school students. "Men are supposed to be big and tough. Women are supposed to be mild and sweet. Gay people sometimes break those stereotypes, and I think that's often what makes people afraid or uncomfortable. But if we let go of what we think people are supposed to be, and we just let them be who they are, we'll see that it doesn't really matter."

 **CLOSE-UP: PEER PRESSURE FUELS STEREOTYPES**

Why do people continue to believe in stereotypes despite evidence that may not support them? Researchers have found that it may have something to do with group pressure. During one experiment, seven members of a group were asked to state that a short line is longer than a long line. About a third of the rest of the group agreed that the short line was longer, despite evidence to the contrary. Apparently, people conform to the beliefs of those around them in order to gain group acceptance.

## "Metrosexuals"

Joe Duarte has experienced the impact of stereotypes first hand. As an attractive, stylish, self-confident, and highly expressive straight man, he's become accustomed to people thinking he's gay just based on the way he looks. After he traded in his company-issued plain black laptop case for a designer leather bag, he was immediately teased by his colleagues.

"My friend said, 'You must be gay. No straight man would carry a bag like that,'" recalls Duarte, who was born in Brazil and relocated to Canada as a teenager. "But why shouldn't guys want to do things like that? It looks better. And it doesn't make me less of a man. My bag or my clothes or my hairstyle have nothing to do with what makes a guy a guy."

His friends often refer to him as "metrosexual"—a straight man who is interested in things traditionally linked to gay men, including shopping, fashion, and grooming. The concept, which is becoming more common in large cities and urban areas, challenges the traditional stereotype that men with effeminate qualities are gay. Duarte's statement implies that to be a gay male would mean he was less masculine—but that's another stereotype! Gay males are just as much "guys" as straight males.

And, as actor Alan Cumming wrote on his blog, "What's wrong with being effeminate? There are loads of straight people in the world who are effeminate. Does . . . society in general have a problem with people who are too *masculine*?"

The stereotypes of what it means to be a man, woman, gay, straight, bisexual, transgender, or anything else limit people from being who they actually are. Practicing tolerance means letting go of those stereotypes and not making assumptions about people.

## Rooting Out Hidden Stereotypes

The Human Rights Campaign (HRC) suggests that individuals and businesses who want to demonstrate tolerance and break down stereotypes should avoid **clichés** that **marginalize** LGBT people.

Even when stereotypes seem like harmless jokes, they can still hurt people. That's why it's important for people to think about the things they say and the assumptions they make.

"It's easy to forget sometimes, especially when you hear other people using those words, how damaging they can be," says Franks. "But when we really think about the way we speak or even the way we think about others, we can start to identify ways that we can remove stereotypes from our vocabulary and from our minds. We can look at people for who they are, not who we think they're supposed to be."

 **TEXT-DEPENDENT QUESTIONS**

- When do stereotypes stop being useful and become harmful?
- How do so-called "metrosexuals" flout (go against) common gay and straight stereotypes?
- What's the most effective way to banish stereotypes from one's way of thinking?

 **RESEARCH PROJECTS**

- What's wrong with being effeminate? Consider what it is about men acting like women that mainstream society might object to.
- Similarly, consider what it is about women acting like men that mainstream society might object to.

# 🔖 SERIES GLOSSARY

**Activists:** People committed to social change through political and personal action.

**Advocacy:** The process of supporting the rights of a group of people and speaking out on their behalf.

**Alienation:** A feeling of separation and distance from other people and from society.

**Allies:** People who support others in a cause.

**Ambiguous:** Something unclear or confusing.

**Anonymous:** Being unknown; having no one know who you are.

**Assumption:** A conclusion drawn without the benefit of real evidence.

**Backlash:** An adverse reaction by a large number of people, especially to a social or political development.

**Bias:** A tendency or preference toward a particular perspective or ideology that interferes with the ability to be impartial, unprejudiced, or objective.

**Bigotry:** Stubborn and complete intolerance of a religion, appearance, belief, or ethnic background that differs from one's own.

**Binary:** A system made up of two, and only two, parts.

**Bohemian:** Used to describe movements, people, or places characterized by nontraditional values and ways of life often coupled with an interest in the arts and political movements.

**Caricature:** An exaggerated representation of a person.

**Celibate:** Choosing not to have sex.

**Chromosome:** A microscopic thread of genes within a cell that carries all the information determining what a person is like, including his or her sex.

**Cisgender:** Someone who self-identifies with the gender he or she was assigned at birth.

**Civil rights:** The rights of a citizen to personal and political freedom under the law.

**Clichés:** Expressions that have become so overused—stereotypes, for example—that they tend to be used without thought.

**Closeted:** Choosing to conceal one's true sexual orientation or gender identity.

**Compensating:** Making up for something by trying harder or going further in the opposite direction.

**Conservative:** Cautious; resistant to change and new ideas.

**Controversy:** A disagreement, often involving a touchy subject about which differing opinions create tension and strong reactions.

**Customs:** Ideas and ways of doing things that are commonly understood and shared within a society.

**Demonize:** Portray something or someone as evil.

**Denominations:** Large groups of religious congregations united under a common faith and name, and organized under a single legal administration.

**Derogatory:** Critical or cruel, as in a term used to make a person feel devalued or humiliated.

**Deviation:** Something abnormal; something that has moved away from the standard.

**Dichotomy:** Division into two opposite and contradictory groups.

**Discrimination:** When someone is treated differently because of his or her race, sexual orientation, gender identity, religion, or some other factor.

**Disproportionate:** A situation where one particular group is overrepresented within a larger group.

**Diverse:** In the case of a community, one that is made up of people from many different backgrounds.

**Effeminate:** A word used to refer to men who have so-called feminine qualities.

**Emasculated:** Having had one's masculinity or manhood taken away.

**Empathy:** Feeling for another person; putting yourself mentally and emotionally in another person's place.

**Empirical evidence:** Factual data gathered from direct observation.

**Empowering:** Providing strength and energy; making someone feel powerful.

**Endocrinologist:** A medical doctor who specializes in the treatment of hormonal issues.

**Epithets:** Words or terms used in a derogatory way to put a person down.

**The Establishment:** The people who hold influence and power in society.

**Extremist:** Someone who is in favor of using extreme or radical measures, especially in politics and religion.

**Flamboyant:** Colorful and a bit outrageous.

**Fundamentalist:** Someone who believes in a particular religion's fundamental principles and follows them rigidly. When the word is used in connection with Christianity, it refers to a member of a form of Protestant Christianity that believes in the strict and literal interpretation of the Bible.

**Gay liberation:** The movement for the civil and legal rights of gay people that originated in the 1950s and emerged as a potent force for social and political change in the late 1960s and '70s.

**Gender:** A constructed sexual identity, whether masculine, feminine, or entirely different.

**Gender identity:** A person's self-image as female, male, or something entirely different, no matter what gender a person was assigned at birth.

**Gender roles:** Those activities and traits that are considered appropriate to males and females within a given culture.

**Gene:** A microscopic sequence of DNA located within a chromosome that determines a particular biological characteristic, such as eye color.

**Genitalia:** The scientific term for the male and female sex organs.

**Genocide:** The large-scale murder and destruction of a particular group of people.

**Grassroots:** At a local level; usually used in reference to political action that begins within a community rather than on a national or global scale.

**Harassed/harassment:** Being teased, bullied, or physically threatened.

**Hate crime:** An illegal act in which the victim is targeted because of his or her race, religion, sexual orientation, or gender identity.

**Homoerotic:** Having to do with homosexual, or same-sex, love and desire.

**Homophobia:** The fear and hatred of homosexuality. A homophobic person is sometimes referred to as a "homophobe."

**Horizontal hostility:** Negative feeling among people within the same minority group.

**Hormones:** Chemicals produced by the body that regulate biological functions, including male and female gender traits, such as beard growth and breast development.

**Identity:** The way a person, or a group of people, defines and understands who they are.

**Inborn:** Traits, whether visible or not, that are a part of who we are at birth.

**Inclusive:** Open to all ideas and points of view.

**Inhibitions:** Feelings of guilt and shame that keep us from doing things we might otherwise want to do.

**Internalized:** Taken in; for example, when a person believes the negative opinions other people have of him, he has *internalized* their point of view and made it his own.

**Interpretation:** A particular way of understanding something.

**Intervention:** An organized effort to help people by changing their attitudes or behavior.

**Karma:** The force, recognized by both Hindus and Buddhists, that emanates from one's actions in this life; the concept that the good and bad things one does determine where he or she will end up in the next life.

**Legitimized:** Being taken seriously and having the support of large numbers of people.

**LGBT:** An initialism that stands for lesbian, gay, bisexual, and transgender. Sometimes a "Q" is added (**LGBTQ**) to include "questioning." "Q" may also stand for "queer."

**Liberal:** Open to new ideas; progressive; accepting and supportive of the ideas or identity of others.

**Liberation:** The act of being set free from oppression and persecution.

**Mainstream:** Accepted, understood, and supported by the majority of people.

**Malpractice:** When a doctor or other professional gives bad advice or treatment, either out of ignorance or deliberately.

**Marginalize:** Push someone to the sidelines, away from the rest of the world.

**Mentor:** Someone who teaches and offers support to another, often younger, person.

**Monogamous:** Having only one sexual or romantic partner.

**Oppress:** Keep another person or group of people in an inferior position.

**Ostracized:** Excluded from the rest of a group.

**Out:** For an LGBT person, the state of being open with other people about his or her sexual orientation or gender identity.

**Outed:** Revealed or exposed as LGBT against one's will.

**Persona:** A character or personality chosen by a person to change the way others perceive them.

**Pioneers:** People who are the first to try new things and experiment with new ways of life.

**Politicized:** Aware of one's rights and willing to demand them through political action.

**Prejudice:** An opinion (usually unfavorable) of a person or a group of people not based on actual knowledge.

**Proactive:** Taking action taken in advance of an anticipated situation or difficulty.

**Progressive:** Supporting human freedom and progress.

**Psychologists and psychiatrists:** Professionals who study the human mind and human behavior. Psychiatrists are medical doctors who can prescribe pills, whereas clinical psychologists provide talk therapy.

**Quackery:** When an untrained person gives medical advice or treatment, pretending to be a doctor or other medical expert.

**The Right:** In politics and religion, the side that is generally against social change and new ideas; often used interchangeably with *conservative*.

**Segregation:** Historically, a system of laws and customs that limited African Americans' access to many businesses, public spaces, schools, and neighborhoods that were "white only."

**Sexual orientation:** A person's physical and emotional attraction to the opposite sex (heterosexuality), the same sex (homosexuality), both sexes (bisexuality), or neither (asexuality).

**Sociologists:** People who study the way groups of humans behave.

**Spectrum:** A wide range of variations.

**Stereotype:** A caricature; a way to judge someone, probably unfairly, based on opinions you may have about a particular group they belong to.

**Stigma:** A mark of shame.

**Subculture:** A smaller group of people with similar interests and lifestyles within a larger group.

**Taboo:** Something that is forbidden.

**Theories:** Ideas or explanations based on research, experimentation, and evidence.

**Tolerance:** Acceptance of, and respect for, other people's differences.

**Transgender:** People who identify with a gender different from the one they were assigned at birth.

**Transphobia:** Fear or hatred of transgender people.

**Variance:** A range of differences within a category such as gender.

**Victimized:** Subjected to unfair and negative treatment, including violence, bullying, harassment, or prejudice.

# FURTHER RESOURCES

**LGBT TV Characters**
An exhaustive listing from GLAAD.
*www.glaad.org/publications/whereweareontv11/characters*

**"Do I Sound Gay?"**
Home site (and trailer) for the award-winning documentary film.
*www.doisoundgay.com*

**American Institute of Bisexuality**
A web community for bisexuals.
*bisexual.org*

**About Transgender People**
Includes definitions, differentiations, and FAQs.
*gaylife.about.com/od/transgender/a/transgender.htm*

# INDEX